Crafts for
Hanukkah

Crafts for HANUKKAH

by Kathy Ross
Illustrated by Sharon Lane Holm

Holiday Crafts for Kids
The Millbrook Press
Brookfield, Connecticut

For Greyson and Allison—K.R.
To Michael—S.L.H.

Library of Congress Cataloging-in-Publication Data
Ross, Kathy (Katharine Reynolds), 1948–
Crafts for Hanukkah / by Kathy Ross ; illustrated by Sharon Lane
Holm.
p.   cm. —(Holiday crafts for kids)
Includes bibliographical references and index.
Summary: Twenty simple projects that kids can make with everyday
objects to celebrate the holiday season. Includes step-by-step
instructions and lists of materials.
ISBN 1-56294-919-5 (lib. bdg.). — ISBN 0-7613-0078-3 (pbk.)
1. Hanukkah decorations—Juvenile literature. 2. Handicraft—Juvenile
literature. I. Holm, Sharon Lane. II. Title. III. Series.
TT900.H34R68   1996
745.594'1—dc20   95-25800   CIP

Published by The Millbrook Press, Inc.
2 Old New Milford Road
Brookfield, Connecticut 06804

Contents

Happy Hanukkah!

Hanukkah is an eight-day Jewish holiday celebration that begins on the twenty-fifth day of the month of Kislev in the Jewish calendar. The first day of Hanukkah is usually in December.

The word Hanukkah means dedication. This holiday remembers the restoration, over two thousand years ago, of a temple in Jerusalem lost to a powerful enemy of the Jews for three years and then reclaimed.

When Judah Maccabee, the leader of a small band of Jewish soldiers, recaptured Jerusalem, he found the temple in ruins. The soldiers immediately cleaned and repaired the temple and relit the menorah, a special branched candlestick holder. According to legend, the soldiers found only enough oil to burn the lamp for one day, but the lamp burned for eight days, long enough for new oil to be made.

Some of the traditions of Hanukkah include lighting a candle on a menorah for each of the eight days of Hanukkah, giving gifts or *gelt* (real or chocolate money), and playing games with spinning tops called *dreidels*. *Latkes,* potato pancakes fried in oil and served with applesauce, is a traditional Hanukkah dish.

The lights of Hanukkah shine to remind us of the miracle of the burning lamp and the miracle of the victory of a small Jewish army, and they celebrate freedom for all Jewish people.

Aluminum Foil Menorah

Light your Hanukkah season with this sparkling menorah.

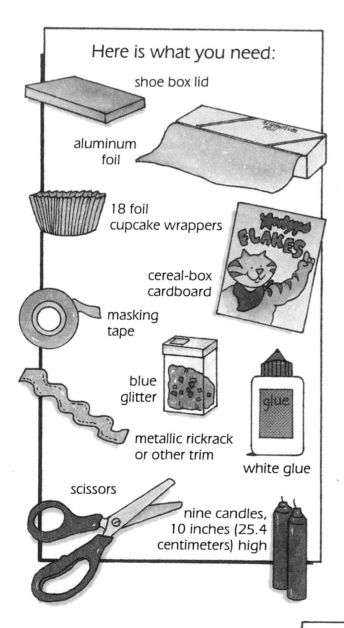

Here is what you need:

shoe box lid

aluminum foil

18 foil cupcake wrappers

cereal-box cardboard

masking tape

blue glitter

metallic rickrack or other trim

white glue

scissors

nine candles, 10 inches (25.4 centimeters) high

Here is what you do:

1. Cut nine circles out of the cardboard. They should be about 1½ inches (3.75 centimeters) wide. Place one circle in the bottom center of a foil cupcake wrapper. Put another foil wrapper inside, on top of the cardboard circle.

2. Put one of the candles in the center of the wrappers and press the sides of the wrappers flat around the cardboard circle and up around the candle. This makes the holder for one candle. You need to make eight more holders.

3. To make the base of the menorah, cover the top and sides of the shoe box lid with aluminum foil. Put a strip of masking tape along the sides of the lid. Cover the masking tape with glue, and then sprinkle the glue with blue glitter. Let the glue dry.

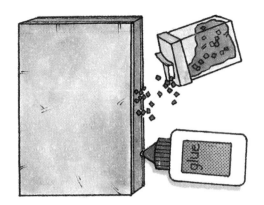

4. Run a line of glue around the middle of the glittered rim and glue on metallic trim. Let the glue dry.

5. A *shamash* is the candle used to light the other candles. Stand the shamash by itself to the far right of the base. Stand the other eight candles in two rows, staggering them slightly. Put a square of masking tape on the base where each candle will stand. Put a square of masking tape on the bottom of each candle holder and some glue on the tape. Glue each candle holder in place on the base and put the candles in the holders.

Place your menorah in a window to remind all who see it of a great miracle.

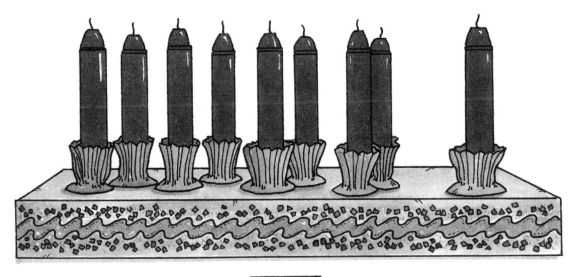

Hanukkah Match Holder

Keep the matches for lighting the menorah
safe and handy with this match holder.

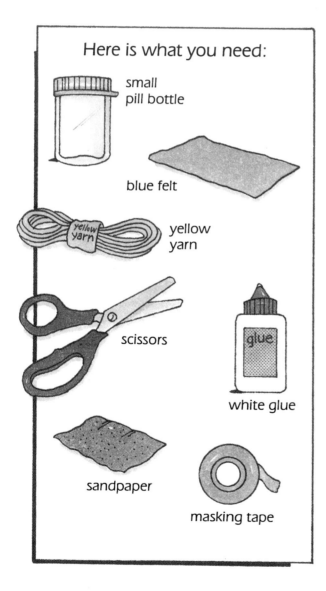

Here is what you need:

small
pill bottle

blue felt

yellow
yarn

scissors

white glue

sandpaper

masking tape

Here is what you do:

1. Cut a piece of blue felt long and wide enough to cover the outside of the pill bottle. The ends should overlap slightly so that you can glue them together.

2. Cut six 1-inch (2.5-centimeter) pieces of yarn and glue them to the side of the holder in the shape of a Star of David. Glue a longer band of yellow yarn along the edges of the felt, at the top and the bottom of the holder.

3. Cut a circle of sandpaper the size of the bottom of the bottle. The sandpaper is used to strike the matches. Glue won't stick to plastic, so you need to put a square of masking tape on the bottom of the bottle before you gluc the sandpaper circle in place.

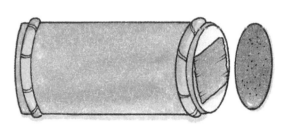

Give this match holder to the grown-up in your house who is in charge of lighting the candles.

Menorah Stabile

A stabile is a type of *standing* mobile. This pretty stabile is a reminder of the lights of the Hanukkah season.

Here is what you need:

large empty thread spool

blue construction paper

gold garland

nine blue pipe cleaners, 12 inches (28 centimeters) long

masking tape

white glue

scissors

newspaper to work on

Here is what you do:

1. Wrap the spool with masking tape. Cover the tape with glue. Then cut a strip of blue construction paper, wide and long enough to cover the spool, and wrap the paper around the glue.

2. Cut nine 1-inch (2.5-centimeter) pieces of garland to use as candle flames. To make each candle, fold each piece of garland in half lengthwise so that all of the strips are pointing in one direction. Make a hook at the end of one pipe

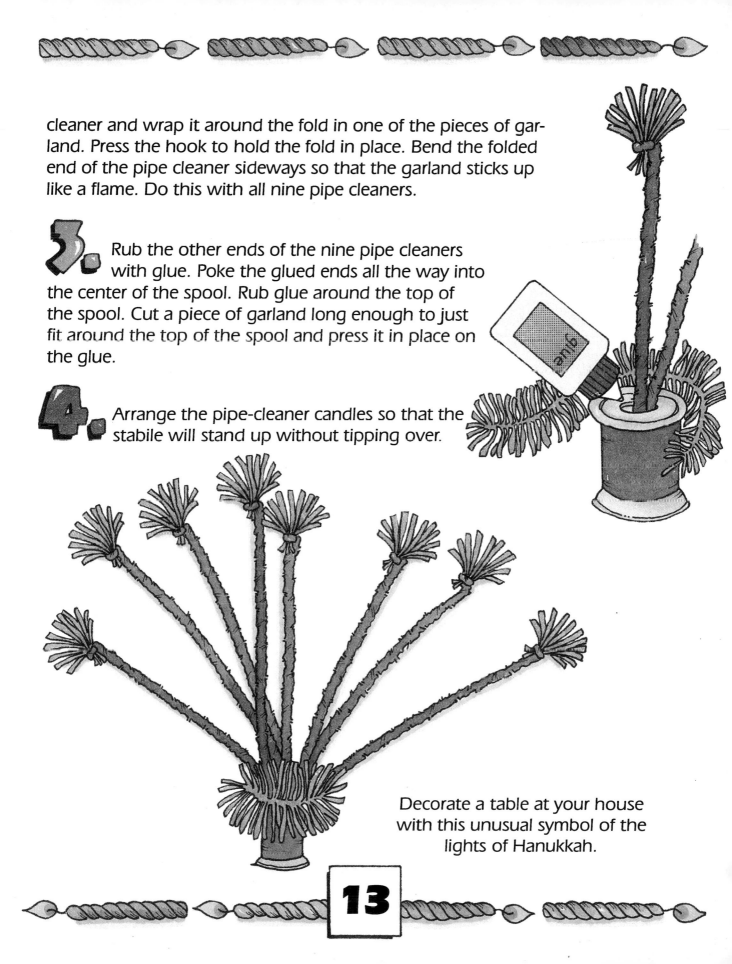

cleaner and wrap it around the fold in one of the pieces of garland. Press the hook to hold the fold in place. Bend the folded end of the pipe cleaner sideways so that the garland sticks up like a flame. Do this with all nine pipe cleaners.

3. Rub the other ends of the nine pipe cleaners with glue. Poke the glued ends all the way into the center of the spool. Rub glue around the top of the spool. Cut a piece of garland long enough to just fit around the top of the spool and press it in place on the glue.

4. Arrange the pipe-cleaner candles so that the stabile will stand up without tipping over.

Decorate a table at your house with this unusual symbol of the lights of Hanukkah.

Gelt Holder

Make this gelt, or money, holder and fill it with chocolate coins to give to young friends who come to visit your house at Hanukkah time.

Here is what you need:

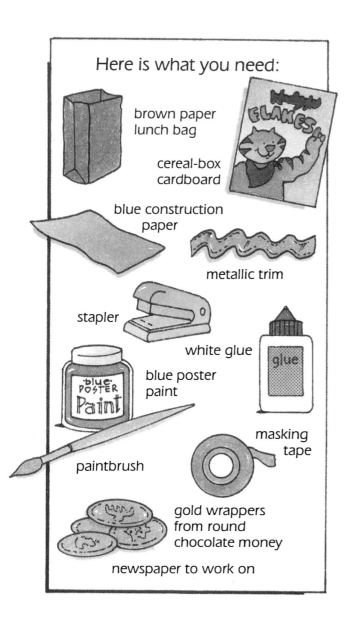

brown paper lunch bag

cereal-box cardboard

blue construction paper

metallic trim

stapler

white glue

blue poster paint

masking tape

paintbrush

gold wrappers from round chocolate money

newspaper to work on

Here is what you do:

1. Cut the top of the bag to make a bag 6 inches (15.24 centimeters) tall. Fold about 1 inch (2.5 centimeters) of the top rim into the bag. Then fold the rim over about 1 inch (2.5 centimeters) again. Cut a rectangle of cardboard to exactly fit in the bottom of the bag to make it sturdy.

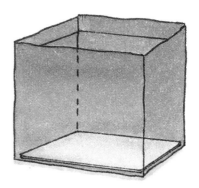

2. Paint the outside of the bag blue and let it dry.

3. Cut a handle about 3 inches (7.5 centimeters) wide from blue construction paper. Fold it twice to make a strong handle that is 1 inch (2.5 centimeters) wide. Glue a strip of metallic trim along the length of the handle, then staple the ends of the handle to the inside of the bag.

4. Fold the edges of the gold wrappers under to keep the coins round. Put a piece of masking tape on the back of each gold coin wrapper. Glue the coin wrappers on all four sides of the holder to decorate it.

Keep the candy-filled holder near your front door to have a treat ready for young Hanukkah visitors.

Latkes in the Pan Game

Hanukkah is the time for eating latkes (potato pancakes) and applesauce. Make this latkes game to play with, not to eat!

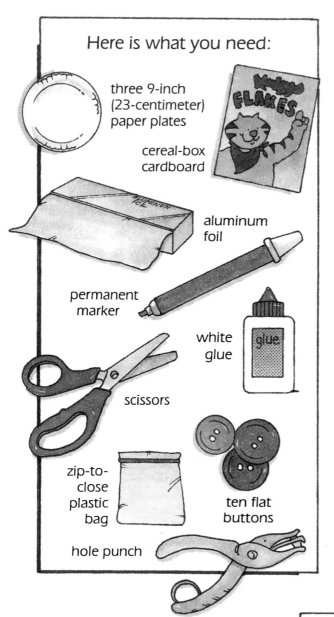

Here is what you need:

- three 9-inch (23-centimeter) paper plates
- cereal-box cardboard
- aluminum foil
- permanent marker
- white glue
- scissors
- zip-to-close plastic bag
- ten flat buttons
- hole punch

Here is what you do:

1. Cut a pan handle about 7 inches (18 centimeters) long from the cardboard. Glue the three paper plates together on top of each other. While the glue is still wet, slide the end of the handle between two of the plates. Let the glue dry.

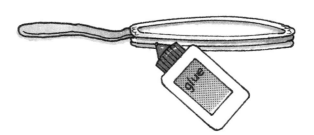

2. Wrap the entire pan in aluminum foil. Use a hole punch to punch a hole in the end of the handle, just like a real frying pan.

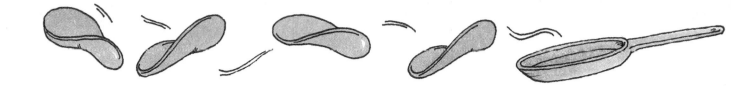

3. With the permanent marker, draw lines inside the pan to divide it into four equal sections. Number the sections 1, 2, 3, and 4.

This game is played like tiddlywinks. Each player uses one of the "pancake" buttons to flip the other buttons into the pan. The score depends on the numbers in the sections where the "pancakes" land.

Store the buttons in a zip-to-close bag when you are not playing with them so they won't get lost.

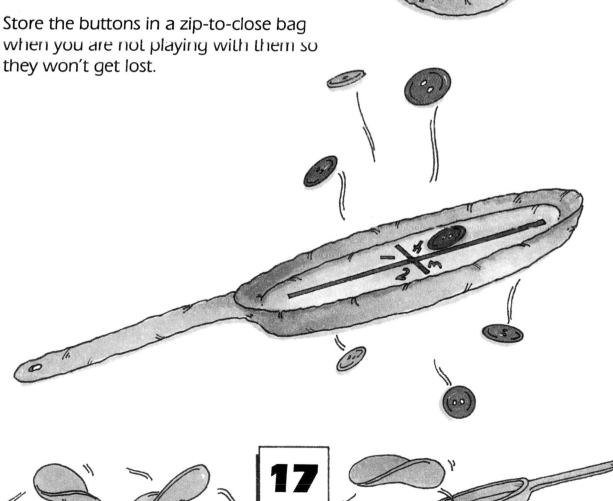

17

Applesauce Jar

Give someone a gift of applesauce to go with their latkes.

Here is what you need:

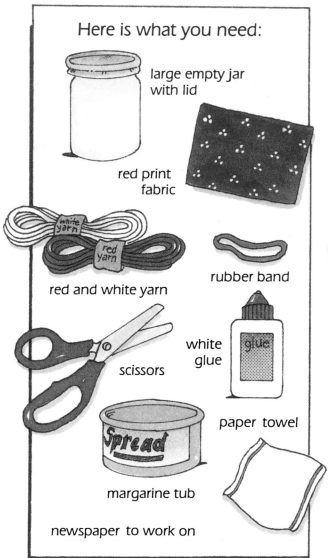

large empty jar with lid

red print fabric

red and white yarn

rubber band

scissors

white glue

margarine tub

paper towel

newspaper to work on

Here is what you do:

1. Cut two apple shapes from the fabric. Also cut a fabric circle that is at least twice as wide as the lid of the jar.

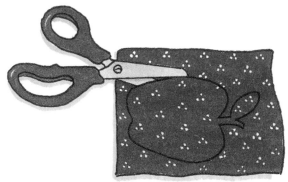

2. Put about ¼ cup (160 milliliters) of glue in the margarine tub. Add about 1 tablespoon (15 milliliters) of water to the glue and stir the mixture with your finger.

Dip one of the fabric apples in the glue and swish it around until it is completely soaked with glue. Squeeze out the extra glue and carefully stick the apple to one side of the jar. Do the same thing with the second apple and stick it on the other side of the jar. Use a damp paper towel to wipe off any extra glue on the jar around the apples. Let the glue dry.

4. Fill this jar with your favorite applesauce and put the lid on. Place the circle of fabric over the lid and hold it in place with the rubber band. Wrap red and white pieces of yarn around the rubber band to hide it and tie the ends in a bow.

What a nice Hanukkah surprise for your family to give to another family.

Envelope Dreidel Card

A dreidel is a four-sided toy, marked with Hebrew letters, that is spun like a top. But this dreidel is not for spinning. It's for delivering a special Hanukkah greeting.

Here is what you need:

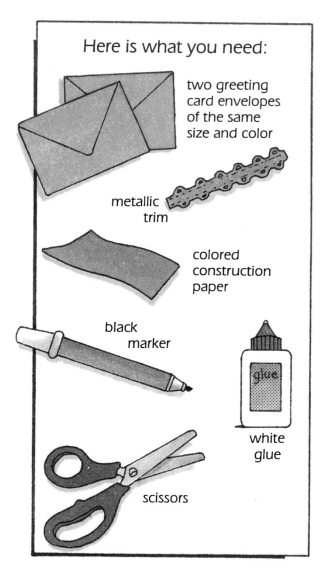

two greeting card envelopes of the same size and color

metallic trim

colored construction paper

black marker

white glue

scissors

Here is what you do:

1. Open the flaps of the envelopes. Put glue along the sides of the back of the envelopes and along the outer edges of the flaps.

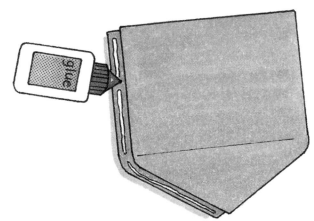

2. With the backs of the envelopes facing each other, glue the flaps and sides together. This will make a dreidel shape with a pocket inside.

   **20**

3. Cut a handle for the dreidel from construction paper. It should be long enough to slide all the way into the pocket to the point of the envelope, leaving a 4-inch (10-centimeter) handle sticking out of the other end. Write your Hanukkah message on the part of the handle that will be hidden. Write PULL at the top end of the handle and slide the message part of the handle into the dreidel pocket.

4. If you used white envelopes instead of colored ones, you may want to color the dreidel with markers or crayons. Draw a Hebrew letter—*Nun, Gimel, Hay,* or *Shin*—on the front of the dreidel with a black marker. Decorate the dreidel and handle by gluing on strips of metallic trim.

Wish someone you know a very happy Hanukkah with this unusual greeting card!

Giant Dreidel

Lean this giant dreidel in a corner of your living room as a fun and different Hanukkah decoration.

Here is what you need:

large, square cardboard carton

cardboard paper-towel tube

blue poster paint

white glue

paintbrush

yellow yarn

masking tape

scissors

yellow construction paper

four clamping clothespins

newspaper to work on

Here is what you do:

1. Bend in the corners of all four carton flaps. Rub glue on the tops of the folded-over portion of all the flaps. Push the four flaps toward the center of the carton with the folded edges inside.

The flaps should be at a slight angle, leaving a square hole at the center. Stick the folded-over triangles to each other. Use clamping clothespins to hold them together while the glue dries.

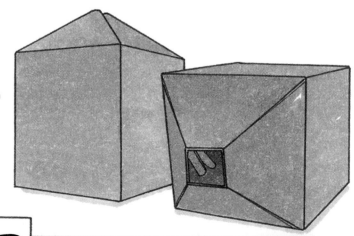

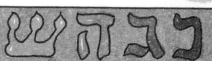

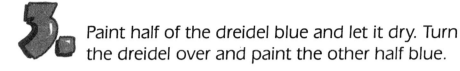

2. Cut four 1-inch (2.5 centimeter) slits in one end of the cardboard tube. Spread the cut tabs out and glue them to the bottom center of the carton to make a handle for the dreidel. Secure them with tape.

3. Paint half of the dreidel blue and let it dry. Turn the dreidel over and paint the other half blue.

4. To decorate the dreidel, paint a band of glue around the top. Cover the glue by wrapping six rows of yellow yarn around the dreidel. Cover the handle with glue and wrap the entire handle with yellow yarn. Cut the Hebrew letters *Nun, Gimel, Hay,* and *Shin* out of yellow paper and glue one letter on each side of the dreidel.

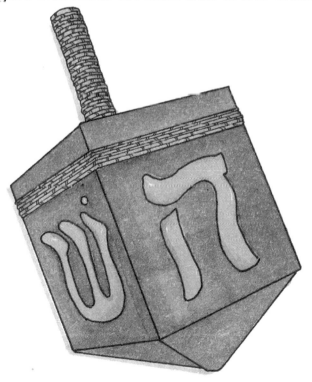

This dreidel also looks great as a centerpiece on a large Hanukkah table.

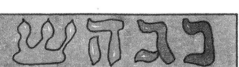

Live Dreidel Game

In this dreidel game, you are the dreidel!

Here is what you need:

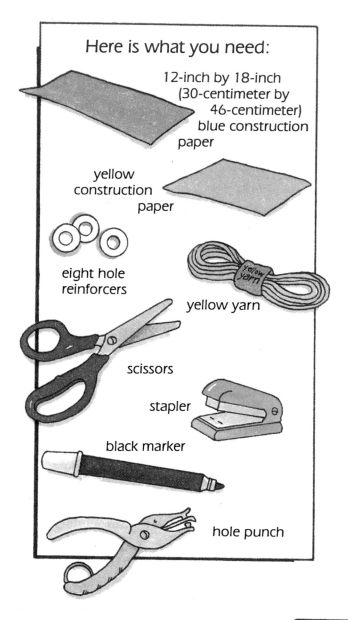

12-inch by 18-inch (30-centimeter by 46-centimeter) blue construction paper

yellow construction paper

eight hole reinforcers

yellow yarn

scissors

stapler

black marker

hole punch

Here is what you do:

1. Fold the piece of blue construction paper lengthwise, leaving 1½ inches (3.75 centimeters) as a single layer along one edge of the paper. Turn the paper so that the single layer is at the top. Cut the paper into four equal sections.

2. Staple the sides of each section to make a pocket. Punch two holes in the top of each pocket, and put a hole reinforcer behind each hole.

3. Cut a piece of yellow yarn long enough to tie around your waist. Weave the yarn in and out of the holes to string the four pockets onto the yarn.

4. Cut a strip of yellow paper narrow enough to fit in each pocket and about 7 inches (18 centimeters) long, so that the end sticks out of the pocket. Write a Hebrew letter near the bottom of each strip. Decorate the outside of each pocket with a Star of David made of two small triangles cut from yellow paper.

To play the game, choose one person to be the dreidel. Another person puts a letter in each of the pockets without letting the "dreidel" see. The dreidel ties the belt around his or her waist so that one pocket is in front, one in back, and one on each side. The dreidel spins around, stops, then falls on his or her front, back, or side, just like a toy dreidel would. Then someone checks the pocket that is facing up to see which letter it contains. Keep score the same way you do when playing with a toy dreidel.

Add some extra fun and laughter to a traditional Hanukkah game.

25

Dreidel Pin

This dreidel won't spin around, but it looks wonderful pinned on a shirt or coat.

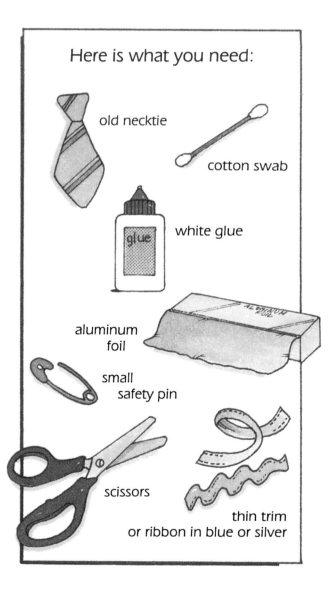

Here is what you need:

old necktie

cotton swab

white glue

aluminum foil

small safety pin

scissors

thin trim or ribbon in blue or silver

Here is what you do:

1. Cut a piece off the narrow end of an old necktie, about 2 inches (5 centimeters) above the point, to make the dreidel.

2. Cut the cotton swab in half. Cover the cotton end of one of the halves with aluminum foil to make a handle for the dreidel. Cover the stick end of the handle with glue. Slip the stick between the front and back layers of fabric at the top of the dreidel.(Glue the fabric at the back of the dreidel together if it came unsewn when it was cut from the end of the tie.)

3. Use narrow trim to make one of the Hebrew letters on the front of the dreidel. Glue one or more rows of trim across the top of the dreidel.

4. Attach a small safety pin to the back of the dreidel so that it can be pinned onto a shirt, jacket, or dress.

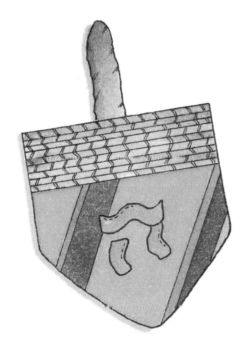

This dreidel also makes a very nice magnet for your refrigerator door. Instead of putting a safety pin on the back, press on a piece of sticky-back magnetic strip.

Kiddush Cup

Wine is drunk from the kiddush cup.

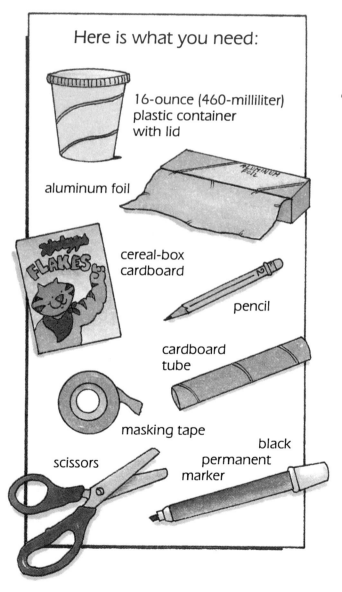

Here is what you need:

16-ounce (460-milliliter) plastic container with lid

aluminum foil

cereal-box cardboard

pencil

cardboard tube

masking tape

scissors

black permanent marker

Here is what you do:

1. Cut a piece of cardboard tube 2½ inches (6 centimeters) long for the stem of the cup. Tape one end of the tube to the top of the lid to make the base. Tape the plastic container to the top of the tube to make the cup.

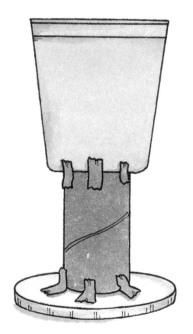

2. On the cardboard, sketch two triangles to make a Star of David that will fit on the side of the cup. Cut out two of these stars and tape them on each side of the cup.

3. Cover the cup with aluminum foil. Cover the base of the cup first. Then line the inside of the cup with a separate piece. Cover the outside of the cup last, carefully pressing the foil over the stars on each side.

4. Carefully outline the stars with a black marker to make them stand out clearly.

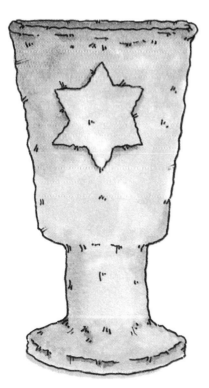

You might have an idea for a different design to decorate your kiddush cup.

Kiddush Cup Necklace

This kiddush cup is to wear.

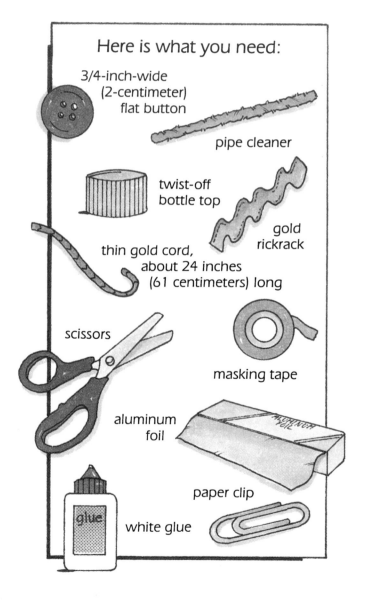

Here is what you need:

3/4-inch-wide (2-centimeter) flat button

pipe cleaner

twist-off bottle top

gold rickrack

thin gold cord, about 24 inches (61 centimeters) long

scissors

masking tape

aluminum foil

paper clip

white glue

Here is what you do:

1. Cut a piece of pipe cleaner 1 inch (2.5 centimeters) long. Bend the tip of one end of the pipe cleaner to the right and the tip of the other end to the left to form hooks.

Tape one hooked end of the pipe cleaner to the center of the button to make the base of the cup. Tape the other end to the center top of the bottle top to make the bowl of the cup.

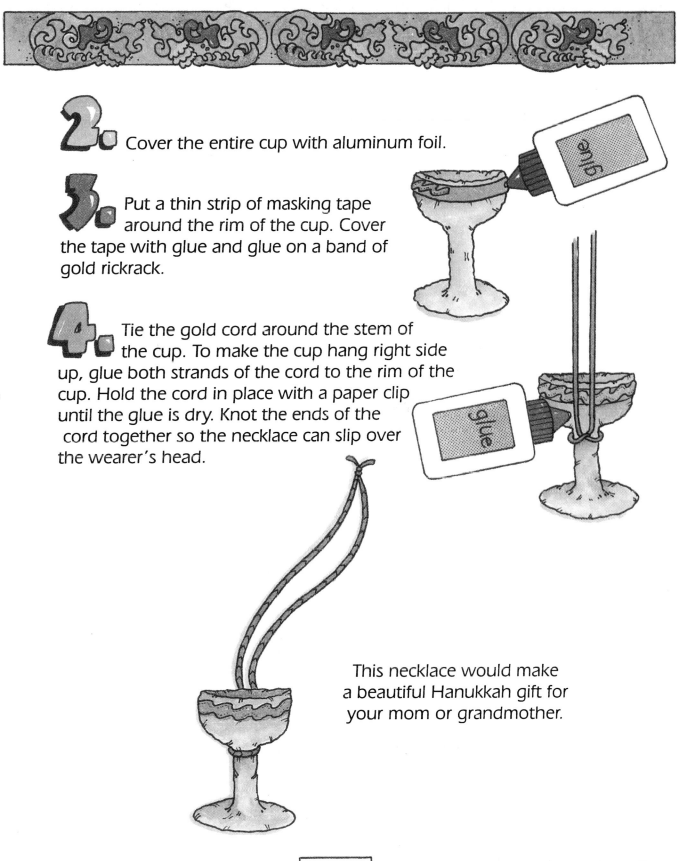

2. Cover the entire cup with aluminum foil.

3. Put a thin strip of masking tape around the rim of the cup. Cover the tape with glue and glue on a band of gold rickrack.

4. Tie the gold cord around the stem of the cup. To make the cup hang right side up, glue both strands of the cord to the rim of the cup. Hold the cord in place with a paper clip until the glue is dry. Knot the ends of the cord together so the necklace can slip over the wearer's head.

This necklace would make a beautiful Hanukkah gift for your mom or grandmother.

Kiddush Cup Door Hanging

Have fun decorating this cup with your own arrangement of colored jewels and glitter.

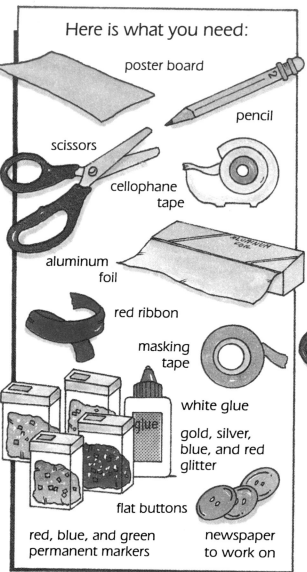

Here is what you need:

poster board

pencil

scissors

cellophane tape

aluminum foil

red ribbon

masking tape

white glue

gold, silver, blue, and red glitter

flat buttons

red, blue, and green permanent markers

newspaper to work on

Here is what you do:

1. Draw a large kiddush cup on the poster board and cut the cup out. Cover one side of the cup with aluminum foil and tape the edges of the foil to the back of the cup with cellophane tape.

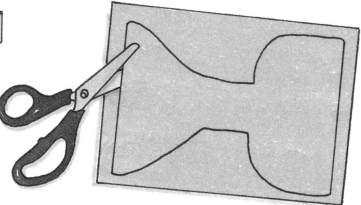

2. Put a strip of masking tape across the cup at each place you would like to decorate the cup with glitter or button "jewels."

3. To make each button jewel, wrap a button with aluminum foil and color the front with one of the permanent markers. Put a square of masking tape on the back of each button.

4. Cover one strip of masking tape on the cup with glue and arrange the jewels on the strip. Sprinkle glitter on the glue around the jewels. Cover each strip with one of the colored glitters or with glitter and jewels. You must work very carefully so that you do not mix different color glitters together on the strip. Let the glue dry.

5. To make a hanger, cut a long strip of red ribbon. Tape the two ends of the ribbon to the top of the back of the cup with masking tape.

This jeweled kiddush cup would look wonderful hanging on your front door.

Doll Yarmulke

Some people wear a yarmulke when lighting the Hanukkah candles.
Make this little yarmulke for a doll friend living at your house.

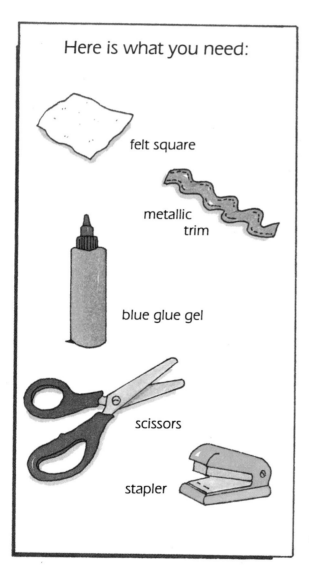

Here is what you need:

felt square

metallic trim

blue glue gel

scissors

stapler

Here is what you do:

1. Cut a circle from felt that is smaller than the head of the doll that will wear the yarmulke.

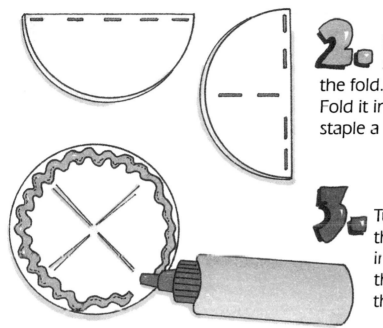

2. Fold the circle in half and staple a small seam close to the fold. Open and flatten the circle. Fold it in half the other way and staple a small seam across this fold.

3. Turn the hat over so that the stapled seams are on the inside. Run a line of glue around the rim of the hat and decorate the hat with metallic trim.

Maybe all of your doll friends should have yarmulkes!

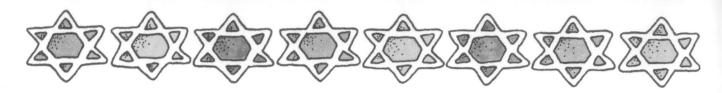

Patchwork Star of David

Ask a grownup if he has some old neckties
you can use to make this project.

Here is what you need:

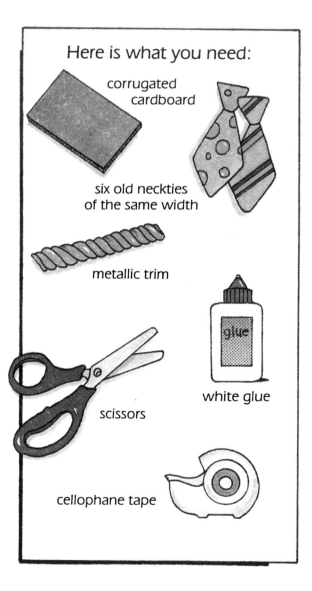

corrugated cardboard

six old neckties of the same width

metallic trim

white glue

scissors

cellophane tape

Here is what you do:

1. Cut the points off the wide ends of six neckties so that you have six triangles. Arrange the six triangles on corrugated cardboard to form the points of a Star of David. Glue the triangles in place.

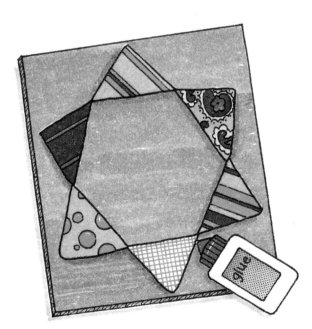

2. From the rest of the necktie fabric, cut more triangle pieces of the same size as the triangle points. Glue them in a random pattern on the cardboard in the middle of the star. Overlap the triangles to be sure that all of the cardboard is covered. Let the glue dry.

3. Cut the star out of the cardboard, cutting as close to the fabric as possible without cutting into it.

4. Cut six strips of metallic trim long enough to go across the base of each triangle point. Glue them in place. Cut a 10-inch (25-centimeter) piece of metallic trim and fold it in half. Glue the two ends to the back of one of the points of the star to make a hanger. Use cellophane tape to hold the hanger in place while the glue dries.

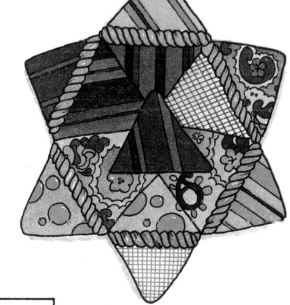

Hang this beautiful Star of David up for everyone to admire.

Star of David Candle Holder

Make a star to shine in your window this holiday season.

Here is what you need:

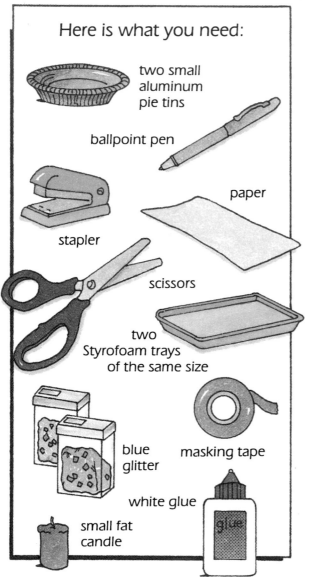

two small aluminum pie tins

ballpoint pen

paper

stapler

scissors

two Styrofoam trays of the same size

blue glitter

masking tape

white glue

small fat candle

Here is what you do:

1. Cut out a circle of paper that will fit in the bottom of one of the pie tins. Sketch a Star of David on the circle as large as the size of the circle will allow.

2. Put two Styrofoam trays under the pie tin to protect the surface you are working on. Use a ballpoint pen to poke holes in the pie tin to outline the shape of the star you have drawn. When you have finished the picture, remove the paper from the pie tin.

3. Cover the sides of the pie tin with masking tape. Cover the tape with glue and sprinkle the glue with blue glitter. Let the glue dry.

4. Tip the pie tin on its side and attach the sides to the lip of a second pie tin with two staples. Stand a candle in the second pie tin. When the candle is lit, turn the pie tin so the light will shine through the star.

Put a small saucer under the candle holder before placing it on the table.

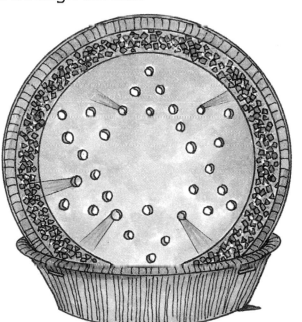

Star of David Mobile

This cluster of stars hangs from the ceiling.

Here is what you need:

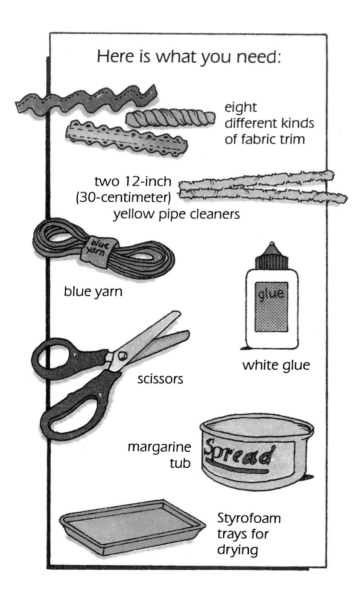

eight different kinds of fabric trim

two 12-inch (30-centimeter) yellow pipe cleaners

blue yarn

white glue

scissors

margarine tub

Styrofoam trays for drying

Here is what you do:

1. To make stars, cut six 3½-inch-long (9-centimeter) pieces from one kind of trim. Pour ½ cup (120 milliliters) of glue into the margarine tub and add a small amount of water to thin the glue.

2. Put all six pieces of fabric trim in the glue and swish them around with your fingers until the pieces are completely covered with glue. Squeeze out the extra glue, then arrange the six pieces on a Styrofoam tray in the shape of a Star of

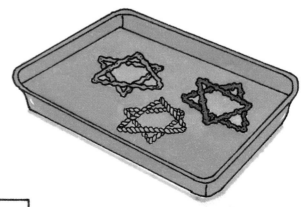

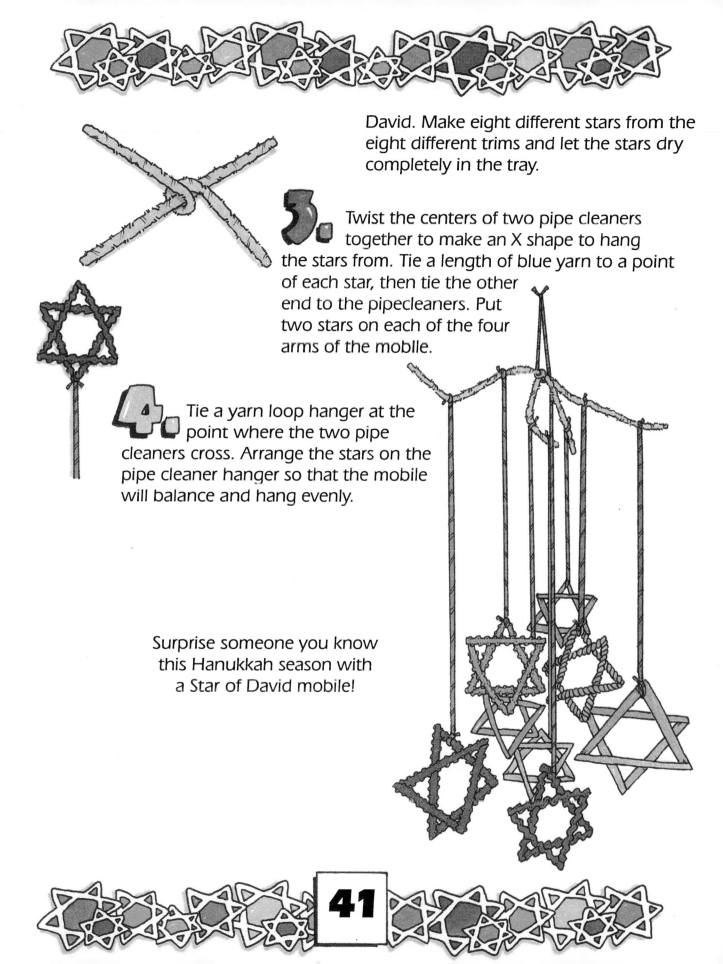

David. Make eight different stars from the eight different trims and let the stars dry completely in the tray.

3. Twist the centers of two pipe cleaners together to make an X shape to hang the stars from. Tie a length of blue yarn to a point of each star, then tie the other end to the pipecleaners. Put two stars on each of the four arms of the mobile.

4. Tie a yarn loop hanger at the point where the two pipe cleaners cross. Arrange the stars on the pipe cleaner hanger so that the mobile will balance and hang evenly.

Surprise someone you know this Hanukkah season with a Star of David mobile!

Maccabee Soldier

Soldiers led by Judah Maccabee recaptured
Jerusalem more than two thousand years ago.
Make your own Maccabee soldier.

Here is what you need:

piece of light-colored
12-inch by 18-inch
(30-centimeter by 46-
centimeter) fabric

permanent markers
in black and
other colors

white
glue

different
fabric trims

scissors

fiberfill

three clamp
clothespins

newspaper
to work on

Here is what you do:

1. Cut the fabric in half. Sketch
the outline of the Maccabee
soldier on one piece of the fabric
with a black permanent marker. (Be
sure to put newspaper down on the
table first because the marker might
soak through the fabric.) Use different colored markers to draw a face
and hair and clothes for the solider.
Glue fabric trim to the clothing.

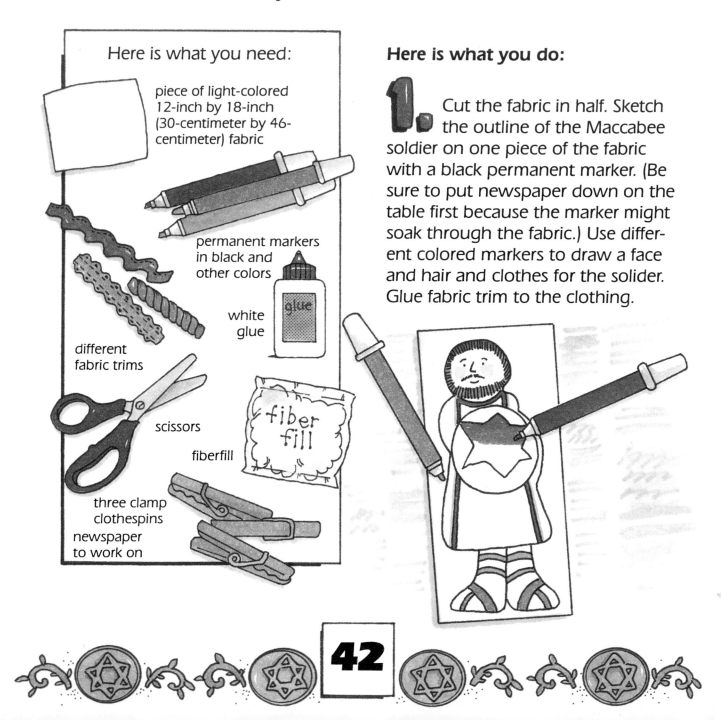

2. Turn the fabric over. You should be able to see the outline of the drawing on the other side. Put glue along the outline on this side, leaving about 3 inches (7.5 centimeters) of the drawing unglued at the bottom so you can put the stuffing in. Set the glued fabric on the other piece of fabric and let it dry.

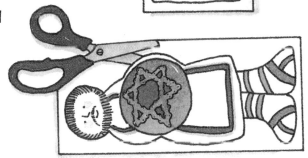

3. Carefully cut the soldier out around the outside of the glued edges. Stuff the doll with fiberfill and then glue the bottom opening shut. Use clamping clothespins to hold the edges together until the glue dries.

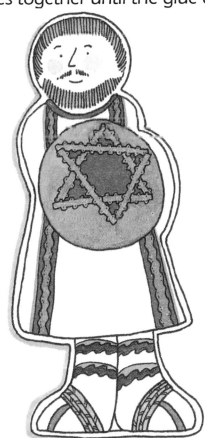

You might want to make a whole group of Maccabee soldiers.

Hanukkah Gift Bags

Gift bags are useful for wrapping your own packages,
or to give as gifts to someone else.

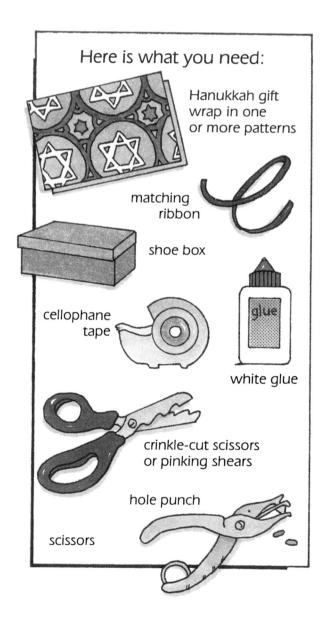

Here is what you need:

Hanukkah gift
wrap in one
or more patterns

matching
ribbon

shoe box

cellophane
tape

white glue

crinkle-cut scissors
or pinking shears

hole punch

scissors

Here is what you do:

1. Cut a piece of wrapping paper the size you need to wrap the shoe box. Wrap the paper around the shoe box. Glue the seam where the two ends of the paper overlap. Hold the glued seam together with cellophane tape. Fold the paper over one end of the shoe box just as you would when wrapping a present. Glue the fold in place and secure it with cellophane tape. Let the glue dry.

2. Carefully slip the paper off the shoe box. You have made a bag! Cut the bag to the height you want it to be, using crinkle-cut scissors to give the top a nice edge.

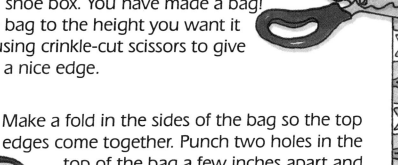

3. Make a fold in the sides of the bag so the top edges come together. Punch two holes in the top of the bag a few inches apart and put a piece of ribbon through the holes. Tie the ends of the ribbon in a bow to close the bag. Do not tie the bow in a knot because the user of the bag will need to open it to put a gift in. You can make gift bags of all sizes by using different size boxes to shape them.

If you remember to save this year's Hanukkah gift wrappings, you'll be ready to make lots of bags next year.

Hanukkah Memory Book

Make a book to keep all your favorite Hanukkah photographs and cards in.

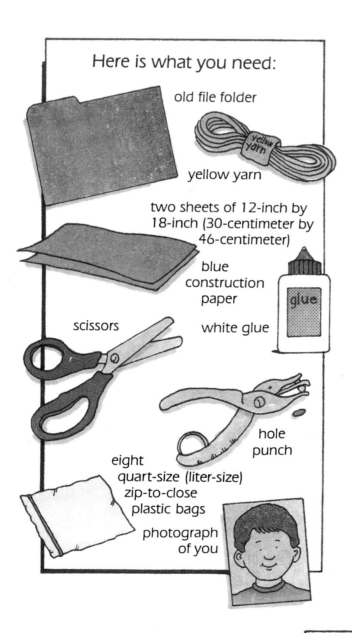

Here is what you need:

old file folder

yellow yarn

two sheets of 12-inch by 18-inch (30-centimeter by 46-centimeter)

blue construction paper

white glue

scissors

hole punch

eight quart-size (liter-size) zip-to-close plastic bags

photograph of you

Here is what you do:

1. If the file folder has a tab on it, trim the tab off. Cover both sides of the folder with glue, and then with blue construction paper. Close the file while the glue is still wet. Trim off any extra blue paper around the file.

2. Before the glue is dry, open the folder and punch holes about 1 inch (2.5 centimeters) apart all the way around the folder. (It will be much harder to punch the holes after the glue is dry.)

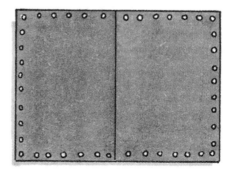

3. Tie one end of a long piece of yarn through a hole at the center bottom of the open folder. Lace the yarn through each hole, wrapping it around the edge of the folder as you go. When you get back to the hole you started with, knot the end of the yarn and trim off any extra.

4. Punch a hole on the foldline at the top and bottom of the folder. Stack the eight plastic bags together and punch a hole on each side of the bottoms of the bags. Run a piece of yarn through the foldline holes and the holes in the bags. Tie the ends of the yarn into a bow on the outside edge of the folder.

5. Cut six 6-inch (15-centimeter) pieces of yellow yarn and arrange them on the front of the folder in the shape of a Star of David. Glue the yarn in place. Glue a small photograph of yourself in the center of the star.

Each year use one of the bags to store your Hanukkah photos and cards in. As the years go by, you can look over your collection of very special Hanukkah memories.

About the author and illustrator

Twenty years as a teacher and director of nursery school programs have given Kathy Ross extensive experience in guiding young children through craft projects. Her craft projects have appeared in *Highlights* magazine, and she has also written numerous songs for young children. She lives in Oneida, New York.

Sharon Lane Holm won awards for her work in advertising design before shifting her concentration to children's books. Her illustrations have since added zest to books for both the trade and educational markets. She lives in New Fairfield, Connecticut.